Volume 7 Issue 2
The Scentual Divinities Issue
www.inspiritmagazine.com

Editor's Note

The Essence of the Divine Feminine inSpires you to love yourself so you are free to love others, it grounds you into your body with its sense of sexuality and, above all, it gives you the freedom to be a woman in all of its glory.

This is also true of the Divine Male, an energy that has been celebrated for centuries, yet is only now coming to an awareness of needing balance between the male and female - the yin and the yang.

This issue we find the Divine Feminine seeking to express itself throughout the pages of inSpirit, and as we come together as a team of contributors, you'll find each of us, along with our special guests, inSpiring you with knowledge and experience gained from having the Divine Feminine show up in each of our lives.

From relationship counselling with Jennifer Granger, Intuition in Business with Simone Malasas, Palm reading inSights with Max Coppa, and an inSightful look at Soul love in the modern world with Amanda Roussety, you will find inspiration to awaken new understandings about yourself and your interactions with others.

This issue we welcome on board two new regular contributors - Toni Reilly whose expertise in Past Life Therapy will fill you with even greater awareness of your Soul Self, while Jude Garrecht, author of Grief to Goddess, will have you celebrating all that you are as you journey along with her.

We are also excited in this issue to not only feature an interview with Dr Steven Farmer, but we are even more excited to be hosting Dr Farmer here in Australia in September for our very first inSpirit #SoulSmile retreat.

#SoulSmile is a weekend of inspiration for the Soul in a relaxed and intimate setting. With numbers limited to just 100 tickets, the potential for connection, change and transformation is high, not to mention how much fun it will be to connect personally with you, our inSpirit community. We sincerely hope you'll consider joining us and making it a weekend to remember.

With love & gratitude, Kerrie

In This Issue

16 Soul Love in Modern Day

3	Finding Yourself Through Your Relationships
4	Up Close and Spiritual: Dr Steven Farmer
6	Self Love - A Soul Conversation
8	Honouring the Goddess
9	Past Lives and the Oldest Profession
10	The Labyrinth
12	Secrets of Release
14	Lost in the Woods
18	Sacred, Sensual, Sexy - The Feminine Power Within
19	Sacred Snake Shifting
20	Love Between the Lines
22	The Sacred Seamstress
24	Nurturing Puppy Love
25	Mystic Elixer of Love
26	The Power of Intuition in the Workplace

Regular Columns

13	Goddess inSpiration
15	Buddhism
15	For the Love of Angels
23	Cosmic Codes
27	inSpirit Reviews
28	inSpirit Directory

25

14

4

9

THE TEAM

MANAGING EDITOR Kerrie Wearing

CREATIVE TEAM Kerrie Wearing, Nicolle Poll, Alex Cayas, Therese Chesworth

EDITOR Nicolle Poll, Therese Chesworth

REGULAR CONTRIBUTORS Kerrie Wearing, Nicolle Poll, Nicola McIntosh, Susanne Hartas, Jude Garracht, Brendan D. Murphy, Gem~mer, Meadow Linn, Alex Cayas, Natasha Heard, Laura Naomi, Kye Crow, Reilly McCarron, Rita Maher, Amanda Coppa, Nicole Humber

GUEST CONTRIBUTORS Danni Stark, Amanda Roussetty, Simone Milasas, Jennifer Granger

GRAPHIC DESIGN Kerrie Wearing, Nicola McIntosh

COVER ARTWORK Nicolle Poll

Finding Yourself
Through Your Relationships
by Jennifer Granger

Charlotte sighed as a reluctant tear fell down her face. "It's true. I didn't realize it, but I do feel like 'the man' around Simon"

We think we know ourselves, until we hit a bump in the road. That "bump" is often caused by an intimate relationship going sour, and suddenly, nothing is clear. We realize that maybe we didn't know ourselves as well as we thought, and our partner seems like a stranger! It is very unsettling, but not at all uncommon.

Here's a new way to look at yourself that will help you keep your relationships in balance. It's best explained by example, so meet Charlotte and Simon. Charlotte was unhappy but couldn't pinpoint what was wrong, other than figuring it must have something to do with Simon.

They had been together for three years and suddenly she felt weary of him. He was so gentle and kind, but so boring, or so she felt. The passion they felt during their first years together was no longer there. In fact, she found he had become unbearably irritating.

When Charlotte and I sat down to chat about her relationship dilemma, she was genuinely at a loss to explain her feelings. After listening to her, I suggested that perhaps she was actually dissatisfied with herself, which at first she strongly denied. But upon reflection, she said, "Maybe. I just don't know, I don't understand. I have a wonderful life, a successful career and I have Simon."

I agreed but posed the question "Yes, but somehow it isn't enough, is it? Something is still missing? It sounds like you love Simon but you are not 'feeling' him the way you used to? You want more from him and he can't give you more? You want to feel more like the woman in the partnership, and for him to be more 'manly'. Is that it?"

She seemed amazed and said "That's correct. But how did you know?" I had a strong hunch because I had seen it so often before. You see, all men and all women have both a feminine and a masculine energy deep within themselves - a yin and yang. When our inner energetic balance is out of whack, within ourselves or out-of-balance in comparison to our partner's energy, then havoc can ensue and intimacy goes straight out the window.

I explained that when they met, they had opposite internal energy and that's what caused the sparks. "You were initially attracted to Simon because he was quite a 'feminine', gentle man. He gave in to your every whim, and now you are finding his attentiveness quite irritating." She nodded sadly.

I continued. "When you met, he was carrying the feminine in the relationship and you fully owned all the masculine energy. You were the one with the big job, the main breadwinner, but now you find yourself empty inside because you are missing your inner feminine essence, plain and simple. You are disgruntled and angry with Simon but he isn't the one who changed. You changed, and it's up to both of you to sort it out."

Charlotte sighed as a reluctant tear fell down her face. "It's true. I didn't realize it, but I do feel like 'the man' around Simon, and I get angry. He is so sweet but I'm still angry."

I reassured her that this could be fixed. In reconnecting with her inner feminine self, she lost the intimate attraction between herself and Simon, because that attraction depends on the two people being internal opposites. When they both were acting primarily feminine, it actually caused the two of them to repel instead of attract.

To correct this imbalance, Charlotte had to realize what was happening inside herself. She explained to Simon that she would really love it if he could step up and be more directive, protective and active, accessing more of his own inner masculine essence. He loved her so much, he did step up. He took on more responsibility for the family financial picture than before and was getting more things done within their relationship.

Once Simon became more masculine in his approach, Charlotte was able to take more time to reconnect with her internal feminine. She began taking personal time to just sit with a cup of tea and think. She joined a yoga class and made time for some girlfriends whom she had neglected when she was too super-busy and too overly masculine in her everyday life.

Fortunately, Charlotte and Simon were able to find a new balance, and each of them felt happy inside. They liked their new roles, and as quickly as the passion had waned it was back again, renewing their wonderful intimate connection.

Jennifer Granger is a transformational coach from Melbourne, Australia and the author of a new ground-breaking book, "Feminine Lost: Why Most Women are Male". In it she explains the sad state of affairs between couples today and explains how creating an internal shift can help individuals attract just the right intimate partner and sustain that love over time.

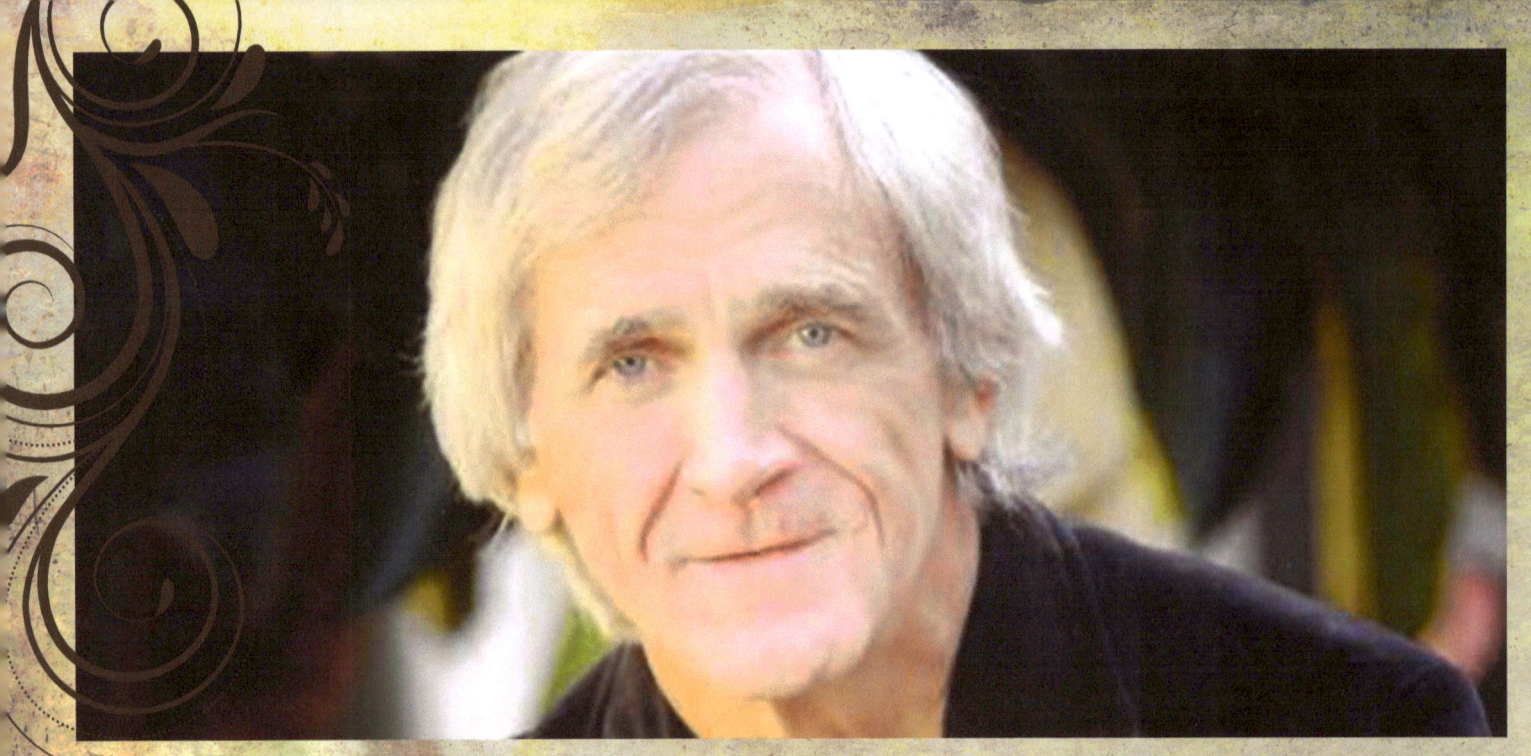

UP CLOSE AND SPIRITUAL

DANNI REMAILI SPEAKS WITH SHAMANIC PRACTITIONER, AUTHOR, PSYCHOTHERAPIST, HYPNOTHERAPIST, SOUL HEALER AND SPIRITUAL TEACHER DR STEVEN D. FARMER TO TALK ALL THINGS SPIRIT, RELIGION AND THE DIVINE FEMININE.

DR: So help us set the scene for the journey we're about to embark on in this interview. I know from our previous interview a while back, I could never forget your ability to ground those who engage in conversation with you and open their minds to life's possibilities. But when and where did it all begin for you? There had to have been a moment, right?

SF: That's a great question and I can think of about 3 different answers. My first one is about 14 lifetimes ago (laughs), but I really think that it began as a child, when I was exposed to religious training or indoctrination. I remember one of my favourite stories about my father, and I was about 5 years old when this happened so it was passed down to me. So he came home one Sunday after going to a Baptist Church and he said "That's it! The Preacher said I can't read the Sunday paper, we're done with that church!"

DR: (laughs)

SF: (laughs) But I like that, you know? It's one of the things I admired about my father, he made a stand. He said, *"That's it you draw the line there!"* But I wasn't really exposed to a lot of religious philosophy, beliefs etc. We did go to church; we ended up going from Baptist to Methodist for a period of time, and Sunday school for a little bit. But I never quite *'got it'*. I've always questioned, *"Is this really true?"* If Jesus is the son of God, then what about the rest of us? But where it really kicked off was after my divorce, and although I had two really beautiful daughters by my side, it really changed me, you know?

DR: Oh it definitely would.

SF: Yeah. So basically I moved into various spiritual belief systems and philosophies. I guess it wasn't a particular event, but a gradual opening. So to put it succinctly, it was a life event of divorce that triggered the change. I went into a stage of seeking. It actually evolved into Shamanism, but that's a whole other story. Once I found Shamanism, I felt very, very much at home.

DR: Well, let's go off from that. For those who have only a brief idea of what a Shaman is, what is the role of a Shaman? I mean, it came at a very important time in your life.

SF: I was a psychotherapist for about 30 years (I mean technically I still am), but once I was introduced to Shamanism I was like *"That's it!"* But I guess the role of a Shaman, and we're hearing more and more about Shamanism, is to mediate the balance between the human community and the natural world. When that is out of balance, the Shaman's first indication is illness in the human community. So his or her role is to seek council or guidance from his or her helping spirits to be able to bring that information to the community, the tribe or the village. So there is a balance between what is received from the natural world and what is given. It's a very earth oriented practice. We work with the earth; we don't just see a tree but a tree with vibration that we call its life force.

DR: I'm making some interesting parallels here with what you've just said. I'm a Secondary teacher, and a student the other day had asked "Why are more people nowadays moving away from organised religion and leaning toward more nature based belief structures?" What are your thoughts on that? I mean, do you think that we have moved away from that restrictive (well, restrictive in my opinion) structure of organised religion?

SF: Well, I think your term 'restrictive' is very accurate, Danni. I mean religious philosophies have served their purpose over centuries, and one aspect of religion has been to provide ethics and direction for the populous. But what I find here is that Shamanism, for example, is about direct revelation, it is not about relying on very old texts. But what I've noticed, and not just those who are doing Shamanic work, but more and more people are finding that they can get information and guidance directly from God/Spirit. Some find they don't need to go to Church to get that, but sure there are some that are more comfortable with the structures you find in organised religion. The second part of your question focused on the earth, which is very immediate and at no cost. But if you research various religions, you'll find there's a value that says something like hey, hang in there, there's a better life when you die.

DR: (laughs)

SF: (laughs) But in all seriousness, I think as a species, we've forgotten our relationship; the intimacy, the connection. I mean not just the philosophy, but heartfelt connection to the other beings of this planet. I mean plants, trees - they're living beings. If they die we die. You can go and put your hand on a tree and you could feel the connection of the life force that's expressing as oneself and as that other being. Back to your question, it's like doctrine without heart. We're forgetting it's a beautiful world, what we have here. It's tempestuous and all the changes that are going on, and we are evolving too. We just can't stay attached to the old ways, including religion (I mean there are a lot of other things) but mainly organised religion.

DR: I completely agree with you on that one. I mean, I know sometimes the ego can get in the way-

SF: Tell me about it. (laughs

DR: (laughs) We'll save that for another interview I think. I want to move onto your experiences with the public, and we really look forward to having you down in Australia very soon. Do you think that location plays a significant role when you're communicating these messages from spirit to those you workshop with? To phrase it better, is a forest better than an office?

SF: (laughs) I don't think it has to matter, no. I mean, I'm sitting in an office; I could step outside and so could you, so could anybody. I don't think people have to go deep into the forest to have that sort of experience of remembering. The opposite of remember is dismember, and we're trying to put it all back together. Identifying more with our consciousness and not with our ego. I don't think it's necessary, but it's definitely easier. It's not that difficult to do. You could meditate, you could imagine a beautiful meadow in your mind, and you don't have to be a Shaman. We are so connected through consciousness, and I love Australia, partly because of the resurfacing of the respect for Indigenous Australians. The respect and acknowledgement that there were ancients here before our forebears came over and took over the land. Not to guilt trip, but it's more a case of "Well now, let's connect to those indigenous qualities." My book, Healing Ancestral Karma, talks about how our ancestors would say "Of course the world is alive!" We just need to become better listeners. Listening with all our senses - our eyes, our ears, our physical being - to what the communication is that's coming through our natural world.

DR: Well let's get specific here. You alluded earlier to the idea of Shamanism and how it doesn't discriminate against gender. Would gender influence the spiritual encounter?

SF: That's a really good question. I think it's not so much gender, but more the feminine and masculine principle. I have, over many years, been involved with men's groups as a participant and facilitator, and I think what I see in the hearts of men is a real desire to do things differently; to show up differently in the world. I think there's something to be said about a good strong masculine love and a respect for the earth. When we take the feminine principle and apply it, it's Mother Earth, as we all know and characterise as feminine. Sometimes we think of the sun as the father/son; bringing the light, so we make those parallels. It's Spring over here, and I just planted some vegetables and I'm loving it. It's a way of honouring Mother Earth.

DR: Perfect segue into my next question. In my research, I found that The Divine Feminine is spread across various cultures and religions, and not just centralised on one particular religion. How do you respond to this?

SF: No, they're definitely not centralised on one particular religion. Even in the Christian religion; Catholicism, Mother Mary is a physical, concrete representative of The Divine Feminine. If you look at the polarities, here's the masculine over here and here's the feminine, human beings in the past and also present, tend to lean toward the masculine. But what I think I've noticed in my research, and you may have too Danni, is that we're coming out of that polarity and into a place of balance where there is more respect for the earth.

DR: You deal with so many people, spirits and energies on a day to day basis, what about Dr Steven Farmer? How do you look after yourself physically, mentally and spiritually? What do you do to stay level headed, so to speak?

SF: First off, exercise and keeping track of nutrition is number one for me. I do my best to eat well, and I do indulge occasionally - you know, chocolate almond bars, something like that. I do cross-fit, that thing taking the world by storm and also Yoga. I keep a balance - there's that thing again, balance. I do eat organic most of the time and I am an omnivore, but I always want to offer a blessing before I eat. It doesn't matter if it's meat or vegetable; they're both living and let's be grateful for that. I, as much as possible, try to be grateful, count my blessings and, whenever possible, get over it!

DR: Perfect advice! To conclude this journey we've undertaken, do you think you chose this journey or your work had chosen you?

SF: I think my soul chose this journey. I'm very clear about that. The soul - sometimes we can connect with it, but the more I go on in my life, the more I'm clear about my soul's destiny. I'm a healer, teacher and communicator, and the form that it is expressed has changed - I've changed. I love my work. I feel very grateful and very blessed to be doing the work that I do - writing, doing workshops and doing private sessions - so that's a really good question Danni. I think that there is some place back behind the mind and the ego that bounces the soul out into the world and that we should continue to get better and better at listening to those inner promptings and those communications both from the visible and invisible realm.

Danielle has a strong affiliation to Parapsychology and the impact of the brain on paranormal experiences. She is a Secondary English and Drama Teacher and Co-host/Researcher/Presenter of Ghosts of Oz on Alive90.5fm

Self Love
A Soul Conversation

Laura Naomi shares with us the beautiful balance of Nature, Shamanism and our own Journey.

> "The most powerful relationship you'll ever have is the relationship with yourself"
>
> Steve Maraboli – author of Life, the Truth, and being Free.

Divine love is the essence of love for all beings, for all of creation. As spiritual beings experiencing this earthly carnation, we get so caught up in loving and caring for others, whether it's our love and support for family and friends, activism for one of the many causes that need highlighting and support, or giving to others through the work we do. This is all very noble, necessary and can even go as far as enriching our soul. Yet, this can, at times come at a big expense. Often we forget to include giving to ourselves in the same way, or simply do not know how. Which was my experience.

I came into this world in less than ideal circumstances, and from a young age felt a need to give love and support to others through their hardships. This in itself is not so bad. However, around this I never really received the same kind of love or validation of who I was in return. Growing up, never feeling loved or supported and learning to take care of what I needed, myself led to developing a life-long behavior of giving and not receiving, and certainly not recognizing where I was receiving love from those close to me.

My life was, and always has been, full of Spiritual abundance. I have not once ever felt unsupported or lacking in love from the Spirit world. My guidance source has always been there and manifested energetically in whatever way was needed at the time for my highest understanding. My guides, Angels or my brother have always been there helping me to grow and evolve through life, even if on the rare occasion they copped a mouthful of frustration from me.

I was, however, often at a loss as to why this didn't transfer through to worldly abundance. Why I was struggling with life in the areas that were important to me, namely my career and business and friendships, and while my home and family was great, there were times when I felt misunderstood and not supported in my life and what's important to me.

Then slowly, last year things began to change. By coming to my knees and finally accepting all that life was, I really began to let go and let God. The funny thing about surrendering is you think you have only to be facing the same challenges once again, but this time I'd finally stripped away to the core of who I was after all of these years, and instead of saying "I need to change or fix who I was, to fix what wasn't working", I came to accept me, my life, and all that that entails and simply began to love all of that. I began to love and give love to myself, as much as I love and give to others.

This was a new learning for me, so to keep myself honest I began a blog of 30 days of Self love which you can find on my website

Doing this saw my life begin to transform immediately. My awareness and how I saw each day shifted straight away, which meant personally I began to feel brighter, happier and coming out of the depression I was in. And it wasn't hard work either, much like affirmation work can be.

I was then guided to new experiences and awareness that cemented new beliefs and behaviours which were better suited to living with this new-found me. They are a whole other article though, some of which was covered in my article Centered in Oneness from our Wholeness and Harmony issue.

Importantly though, the real key to transforming life was to focus on my daily choices and align them with not only what was important for me, but to ensure those choices incorporated a sense of serving myself as much as I serve or give to others. For me this meant formally sitting down and writing out a list of daily choices, but for you it may mean a simple shift in awareness, to honour any soul urge you feel and begin to have a real conversation with your Soul.

In real terms, this means the next time you feel an urge to go and Meditate, to sit in Solitude, to heal, to dance or to say no, do it!

We get so caught up in "Oh I will, but I need to do this first." "This" being taking care of the kids, preparing dinner, your to do list, or anything else you want to insert in place of "this". What usually occurs next is that we never get around to connecting with our Soul, because life has gotten in the way. Then before too long the cycle keeps repeating itself and the Soul eventually goes quiet, giving up and receding into ill health, while we leave ourselves mentally asking for help and for guidance from Spirit.

Loving yourself first does not mean being selfish. Far from it. You are in essence giving to yourself so you can then continue to give to others, to be the best you can be for others, and showing the important people in your life that you matter, and more importantly, teaching them to love themselves too.

While making a change of this nature can be hard to do for some people, it is just a matter of making a mindset change. Be mindful of incorporating some form of self love in your day, every day, and allowing yourself to honour your Soul's urges.

This will naturally result in life taking on a greater flow of ease and grace, as it did for me. Very quickly I found that doorways began to open, where I had often been banging my head up against a brick wall or going around in circles completely dissipated. And more importantly, I began to see the universe supporting me in much more physical ways.

In April of this year, I was granted the most wonderful opportunity to work on Hay House Radio with John Holland on his show "Spirit Connections". This opportunity didn't come along because I needed to 'learn' some thing, like so many previous opportunities. It came because for the first time I was open to receiving love and support and someone was willing to give without expecting anything in return.

Kerrie Wearing is an internationally recognised Soul Coach and Medium, specialising in coaching and mentoring people to connect with their unique Soul Purpose. She is the author of A New Kind of Normal; Unlock the Medium Within, managing editor of inSpirit Magazine and director of inSpirit Publishing. Website: www.kerriewearing.com

Honouring the Goddess

Brendan D Murphy gives us some inSight here with his interpretation of the legend of the While Buffalo Calf Woman

"A man who looks first to a woman's outer beauty will never know her beauty divine, for there is dust upon his eyes and he is as good as blind. But a man who sees in a woman the Spirit of the Great One, and who sees her beauty first in spirit and in truth, that man will know God in that woman; and should she choose to lie with him, he will share with her in enjoyment more fully than the former ever could. And all will be as it should. If you seek first the sacred vision of the Great Spirit, you will see as the Creator sees, and in that seeing, you will find that what you need from the earth will come readily into your hands. But if you seek first to secure your earthly desires and forget the Spirit, you will die inside."

So spoke the mysterious White Buffalo Calf Woman to a young warrior brave of the Sioux tribe, according to Ken Carey's channelling in Return of the Bird Tribes. Her words were at once a confirmation, a reminder, and a warning to the young man not to subvert the calling of his spirit to the whims of the ego and the flesh, as his deceased friend had done just moments earlier, before being turned - in a matter of moments - into a rotting corpse. Ruled "ever by his passions", the unfortunate lusty Sioux had forgotten not only the Great Spirit, but his own spirit as well. He contributed nothing of meaning to the White Buffalo Calf Woman (the Great Spirit incarnate) who satisfied his lust, nor to womankind or his people at large, thanks to his preoccupation with sense gratification. He was "dead inside" and could only offer what he himself sought: pleasures of the flesh and no more.

We men must ask ourselves in this age of transition what we wish our legacy to be when we leave this earth: something of meaning; a life filled with purpose - or mere empty acquisitiveness, hedonism, and a reputation for knowing how to have a good time?

When we look not simply to gain a few moments of entertainment or titillation from a woman, but make the choice to see behind the outer visage to the essence that animates it, we create the opportunity to honour the Great Spirit inside her that animates all - including ourselves. Suddenly the chance for a meaningful connection arises, and more than that: a reconnection to ourselves. We are encouraged all day, every day, by the mass media and a sexually charged culture to see nothing but the surface layers of who we are. Sex sells and everyone seems to be buying. The conditioning is thick and omnipresent. How any male in his twenties or beyond ever manages to make a meaningful connection to a female for the greatness she is within, when we males are ever cajoled into seeing women merely as empty vessels, seems a miracle to me.

It took me a little while to start breaking through that conditioning, but I find myself now, at age 30, in a life situation with a partner who I see as so much more than a nice arrangement of alluring curves. She is the Goddess incarnate to me, and I honour that, and cannot even begin to compare the contentment and gratitude that flows from having such a connection to someone, with the empty and temporary gratification that comes from having an attractive "trophy partner", someone you think you should be with because they will make you look "good" or "successful" or "appealing" - a status prop in other words.

Every woman has an inner goddess. When I look for that and see that she honours and respects herself in awareness of her divinity, I am drawn in - it is a very attractive quality that transcends mere appearances. As a conscious man in awareness of his own Spirit, a sexual union with the Goddess incarnate is something beautiful, transcendent, and, paradoxically, it may seem to some, spiritual. There is nothing that compares.

So, fellow blokes, I invite you to redirect your self-serving inclinations towards women slightly if you haven't already: man up, be "selfish", and find one who embodies the Goddess. Learn who she is, connect with her divinity - and yours - and laugh together. You'll wonder why you waited so long to look a little deeper - and then you'll thank me.

When you honour the goddess, she will honour you.

Brendan D. Murphy is a researcher, speaker, musician, and the author of The Grand Illusion: A Synthesis of Science and Spirituality – Book 1 (TGI 1), described by author Sol Luckman as a "masterpiece." Brendan is also a certified Psych-K facilitator, a certified DNA Potentiator (Potentiation is the first DNA activation in Luckman's Regenetics Method) and has received formal EFT training (levels 1 and 2). The Grand Illusion—along with free book excerpts and articles—is available at www.brendandmurphy.net.

Past Lives and the Oldest Profession

Toni Reilly regales us with how our Past Lives can and do inSpire us in this life.

If you have a perception of what Past Life Regression is, you might find it to be different. Some have told me it is dredging up the past, and ask why you would do that, with the rationale to leave the past in the past. It is far from dredging up the past just for the sake of it.

Regression targets the core incident or experience which attributes or is responsible for triggering behaviours, feelings, fears, reactions or physical symptoms which do not make sense. During regression some go to earlier in current life, others go into the between life phase which is when our soul is not in a body and find their answers there. These areas are as valid as finding healing within in a past life. In each issue of inSpirit I'll talk about cases which have experienced profound results using past life regression.

The reason that past life therapy is so efficient for healing is because each person who delves and discovers past memories can rest assured that the soul, their higher-self, has guided them to the event or experience which holds insight and answers they are seeking.

This issue of inSpirit Magazine is featured around the divine feminine, and to look at this within past lives I want to talk about the oldest profession. It comes up at times during regression. I have had clients tell me that they work as a dancing girl, a working girl, a prostitute or in a harem, and not once has the issue for them related to the fact that they survived by use of their feminine charms.

In a case where my client said she worked in a saloon as a prostitute, we explored what that was like for her - she was happy; and she had good friends, singing, dancing, drinking and partying and leading a merry life. Charming the men who passed through was not degrading for her - she told me it was fun, she enjoyed her life. In her case we did not discover any mistreatment and she did not feel disrespected or ashamed of herself. In fact, she was well off and able to support herself and family members by entertaining those who sought her feminine charms.

Her issue began when she fell in love with a man. He did not want her working with other men and insisted she stop and lead her life as his dutiful wife.

Her husband forced her to behave as he wanted her to and that did not include frolicking with friends and certainly not as a party girl, flirting with or entertaining other men. The marriage turned sour, leaving her trapped in a desperately unhappy life of physical and emotional abuse. Her husband claimed she owed him for saving her from her dreadful life. She felt obligated to his demands, his expectations of how she should behave and the rest of her life was miserable. Her oppression was not from her life as a working girl but from living a lie, and denying the fun loving side of herself - the social side, the girl who loved being with her friends, the girl whom she really was.

My client came searching for why she stayed in an oppressive and unfulfilling relationship with her husband in current life. She understood that her lesson in the past life was to learn how it felt to be controlled by another, to lose her sense of personal value, to live for someone else, and endurance, and that she did not have to relive those circumstances this time around. Following the session my client felt empowered to alter her current situation.

Regardless of your choice of career, nurture yourself, be the person you really are. Bending and swaying in a way that someone else expects is denying yourself the freedom to be the real you. Women, by nature, are usually innately soft hearted and we mother and nurture. That is the essence of feminine energy. You will benefit from directing your divine femininity at yourself as you need nurturing, kindness and acceptance, and this applies to both men and women as we all have a degree of soft feminine energy within us.

Toni Reilly is an internationally recognised Past Life facilitator and professional trainer. After training with Dr. Brian Weiss she devised her own unique techniques. As the founder of Toni Reilly Institute she developed the Diploma of SoulLife™ Psychology, a professional qualification for intuitive practitioners.

www.tonireillyinstitute.com | www.tonireilly.com.au | info@tonireilly.com.au | + 61 0413 088 970

The Labyrinth

Jude Garrecht steps the path of her own personal Labyrinth journey, gently and purposefully taking you with her to connect to the very heart of its centre and to the Divine Feminine mother, the Goddess, that awaits us all there...

I walk the rocky Labyrinth; head down, contemplating my footfalls, mindful as I place one foot in front of the other. My heart is open to the messages I know will come from Mother Earth, the epitome of the Divine Feminine – THE ultimate Goddess who loves me unconditionally and universally.

Moments before, I had stood at the entrance to my recently and lovingly constructed Labyrinth and asked for guidance for the next step on my life journey. I am beginning a new chapter in my personal life story as an author AND a loving partner in a new relationship and I know this Goddess, this powerful embodiment of the Divine Feminine will guide me well as I write the next chapters.

I am establishing new goals as I settle into my new life. My own inner Goddess has intuitively set them in place. Whenever I consciously connect with Gaia I am rewarded with messages for taking the next steps or perhaps revisiting an old step or finding a way around an obstacle that has appeared in my life. These messages come through images or an instinctual knowing as I walk my labyrinth or, more often than not, symbolically through my dreams.

The Goddess has served me well on my journey thus far; I live the life of my dreams. She has taught me how to connect deeply with her and find my way forward through her Divine Guidance. The lessons and challenges I traverse on my path are tempered with her nurturing embraces when the going gets tough.

I am connected to her as she is to me. I work with her daily. I talk with her, I listen and I offer love and gratitude in return. Today, my resident eagles soar above me, calling to me as I walk this Labyrinthine journey. My Labyrinth is grounding and filled with powerful intent to connect my core with the core of the Goddess.

Meditative waves of peace fill me to overflowing. Each step keeps me mindful of my journey inward. The Goddess awaits.

The centre of my Labyrinth is buzzing with the power of my connection to our Divinely Feminine mother; the Goddess.

Who is the Goddess; what is the Divine Feminine? How many times do we research her without coming up with an adequate and definitive answer? The Divine Feminine exists within us all. We are not special; we are not unique in this regard. The vibration of the Divine Feminine is available to everyone – without exception. So why don't we tap into that innate part of us every single day? Why do we think the Divine Feminine is something to be attained outside of us? Perhaps the answer lies in our perceptions of our worthiness.

Do we feel worthy of being fully embraced by the Divine Feminine? Do we think this connection belongs only to a select group? Do we feel that the life that is external to us is more important, as well as all consuming, than to explore the beauty we know exists but have yet to tap into? Do we have the time, resources or the ability to simply be in our Divinely Feminine power? Do we think we have to create a sacred space or meditation time to connect with this power?

The Divine Feminine is beautiful, she is a rich tapestry of life experiences, she is vivacious, intelligent, sexy, unique, ballsy, brash, humble, intuitive, and purposeful and so many other things that will be uncovered as we traverse this journey called life. She is you, she is me and she is a part of us. We are one! Can't see yourself as any of the above? Well, you are EVERY one of those aspects of the Divine Feminine and more.

We often forget that we have this part of us that says, 'shoulders back girl, this is your time to step into your Divinely Feminine power'. Stuffing it down is not the same as denying the existence of it in your life. You may have already faced seemingly insurmountable challenges in your life but stuffing your Divine Feminine power down deep inside you only delays the inevitable as we are all challenged at different times to step up and be in your personal power and live the 'authentic' life you were destined to live. The longer you ignore the existence of your personal Divinely Feminine power, once it has surfaced into your consciousness, the more the challenges will seek you out to ensure you look at your old and outworn stories and grow into the person you were destined to be – warts and all (my favourite saying!).

Being in denial of the existence of the Divine Feminine will also bring its challenges. These challenges may take the form of a 'dark night of the soul' as you are pushed, nudged or dragged into being your Divinely Feminine persona. The Goddess knows your courage and your strength. She will hold you close in her embrace and ultimately thrust you forward, knowing that your courage and your strength are the swords you carry to cut away your attachment to your old stories. She knows, without a shadow of a doubt just what you are capable of achieving.

Imagine how powerful simply acknowledging that part of you, the part that is so deeply and Divinely Feminine that you begin to realise that you are living your life beyond your wildest dreams, your greatest imaginings – one small step at a time. You are writing a new and powerful creative chapter in your life story.

This power connects with the Divine Feminine power of The Goddess that we walk with in this life. She recognises her daughters and her sons and breathes a sigh of contentment. The more you connect with her, the more she will feed you and nurture you and show you how to get the very best out of this lifetime.

You will feel your own power. You will feel your innate inner beauty. Your vivacious nature will come out in the way you express yourself. This may be through writing, art, cooking, your work environment, your interpersonal relationships, parenthood, your career or through all manner of ways. You make decisions based on your connection with the Divine Feminine – which is instinctively YOU!

She is not outside of you – she IS you, in all your glory! Be connected, love who you are. Express yourself creatively in your Divinity.

By walking in my own Divinely Feminine power I create my life in so many different ways. The life I have always known existed for me (and yet didn't how it was going to manifest) is now mine. The goals I set for myself are now my reality. How? By being connected to The Goddess as the face of the Divine Feminine wherever I have lived – the mountains in a sometimes dark cycle of learning, the ocean as a single middle aged woman on her healing journey and now on a mountain top with my beautiful life partner, my dog, cats, abundant wildlife and my creative spirit.

Sometimes I walk my Labyrinth to connect my innate Divinely Feminine self with The Goddess, sometimes I sit at my computer and write, sometimes I bake biscuits or make love or read or stack wood. I am connected to my Divine Feminine power in every way, every day. There doesn't need to be a separation to connect. This is true for everyone. You connect with your Divine Feminine in whatever way feels beautiful and sensual and loving for you. It is a state of being that just is!!!!

For the past 18 years I have created ceremonies and meditations and programs for connecting deeply with Gaia and she has heard and felt my deep connection to her. I stepped up and into my Divinely Feminine power. I tapped into my worthiness, my inner beauty, my vivacious, sexy, intelligent self and I lived and continue to live and love 'on purpose'. I trust the journey even when the going gets tough on occasion. When I have 'had enough', I am human and I throw tantrums and rant at the forces that deeply challenge me. Then, when I am done (usually only a short interlude), I surrender to The Goddess and her wisdom. The Goddess encourages me to return to being 'on purpose'. My purpose is to encourage others to live 'on purpose'; to connect to their own Divine Feminine and the Divine Feminine that is The Goddess to 'Seed their Dreams and Live their Goals' as they write the next chapter in their life story. This is a big part of my creative journey to connect with The Goddess on my journey into my labyrinth today.

Finally, after each twist and turn, I reach the centre. Sitting on the seat created especially for the purpose of deep contemplation, I look out at the view over the gum trees and mountains beyond. I look to the ground under my feet and see the rich soil surrounded by the rocks of the labyrinth and the crystal I placed in the power point of this central location.

I feel The Goddess beneath my feet as the loop of energy begins to circulate between us. I am at peace as my messages begin to flow. I am her, the Divinely Feminine Goddess who is Gaia and she is me. We are one.

Jude Garrecht, author of 'From Grief to Goddess' book and Healing Cards, is passionate about helping others access their inner realms to write new chapters in their life story. Jude's intimate connection to Mother Earth and the messages that come from nature weave a path in the unity between mind, body, soul and emotions to form the foundations of her business 'Dreaming the Seed' and her formula for successful goal creation.
Jude's workshops, programs, readings, meditations and ceremonies for transformation take you on a deep journey of self; evoking peace, contentment and wellbeing. These journeys encourage you to take your personal visions into your everyday life to blend spirit and substance; to move with the cycles of our ever-changing world. Jude is a Psycho Spiritual Hypnotherapist, a Colour Therapist and Clairvoyant. Contact Jude at: Web: www.dreamingtheseed.com & www.fromgrieftogoddess.com

Secrets of Release

IT IS NO SECRET THAT WE ARE CREATURES OF DESIRE. We somewhat forget at times that we are here to enjoy life and what it has to offer. When did you last experience desire or sensuality? While we all seem to be striving for spiritual awareness, we seem to forget about our earthly life. Many work with their higher chakras, trying to obtain higher and higher states of being and enlightenment. But in reality, we are already spiritual beings, we are here to learn about our earthly states of being. One can work with the lower chakras just as much as the higher and still obtain that high sense of awareness. Even more so at times, because our energy will then be deeply rooted in the earth, which allows us to use our wisdom gained in a very grounded and confident way. I am by no means saying that one is better than the other and there really is no separation, we should be working on all our chakras in a balanced way. I am merely stating not to overlook the lower chakras, as they also have very significant importance.

Each chakra is related to a specific set of lessons to learn on earth.

If we experience trauma within each life lesson that relates to a particular chakra, we can inhibit the flow of this chakra and with anything you inhibit the flow of, you will ultimately create dis-ease in that area or its surrounds. Thus, it is not only important to seek medical advice at times, it is equally important to work through the psychological and emotional issues that you may be harboring, holding onto or avoiding. Holding onto emotions is like crimping a hose. The water will bank up behind the crimp and create more and more pressure. The point to working with your chakras is to let the energy flow in a state of balance, which results in a feeling of happiness and centredness.

As we grow and go through different stages in life we learn the lessons of each chakra in order, starting with the Base Chakra. The Base Chakra according to Caroline Myss PhD, in her book Anatomy of the Spirit, states that 'The first chakra grounds us.' It is where we learn of our sense of family. But not only that, 'it also connotes group identity, group force, group willpower and group belief patterns.'

The Sacral Chakra according to Caroline is specific to The Power of Relationships. Caroline claims that 'illnesses that originate in this energy centre are activated by the fear of losing control.' This fear can be financial, sexual, addictions, abandonment etc.

Any imbalance in the Sacral Chakra due to fear can also inhibit the wonderful energy that is expressed through this chakra, like sexuality and creativity.

When you choose an activity that works directly with a specific chakra, it can help remove blockages or issues imprinted in that chakra as a positive side effect. Just like if you suppress your creativity, it will have a negative effect on your sacral chakra. Sometimes you don't need to know or understand what issue has affected it, you can just work on the chakra if you understand what each chakra represents i.e. if your creativity is blocked - work with this chakra. If you have issues with expressing your sensual side or have issues with passion or intimacy - work with the chakra. So how do you work with this chakra? The Sacral Chakra is Orange. Surround yourself with orange, eat orange foods, wear orange clothes. Do something creative! I tend to use crystals. It's good to spice it up and use a variety of things, but I always come back to crystals.

I have created the crystal grid (shown) as an example to 'activate' the Sacral Chakra. If you have excess in this chakra already (i.e. excessive sexual drive) I would opt for making a grid using different stones to calm it down with emeralds of any colour or green stones. For this grid I chose all Orange Calcite, Golden Calcite and Quartz. You can create your own grid or you can meditate on this image. If making your own grid, go with what your intuition says. There is no right or wrong. Grids only help to amplify your own intention anyway, so if your intent is to work with your Sacral Chakra, then ultimately that is what your grid will do.

Use whatever meditation method works best for you. You may wish to picture the grid being absorbed into your body or the energy flowing out into the room you are in so wherever you go you are in the energy of the grid. You might want to put the picture up somewhere where you are likely to see it all day.

I WOULD LOVE TO HEAR FROM YOU ABOUT YOUR EXPERIENCES WITH WORKING WITH THIS GRID!

Feel free to contact me through my website: www.spiritstone.com.au. You can also sign up for my newsletter and as a special gift you will receive a FREE Crystal Grid Template to download so you can get started right away!

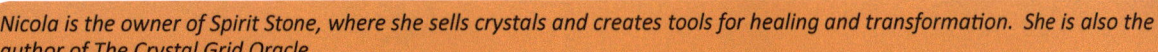

Nicola is the owner of Spirit Stone, where she sells crystals and creates tools for healing and transformation. She is also the author of The Crystal Grid Oracle.

Contact Nicola at www.spiritstone.com.au / https://www.facebook.com/SpiritStoneCrystals

Artwork Credit: Nicola McIntosh

GODDESS INSPIRATION

Rati- HINDU GODDESS OF LOVE AND PASSION

The word Rati refers to anything that can be enjoyed, however it is mostly used to refer to sexual love.

Rati was said to be extremely beautiful and sensual. A very feminine Deity. She was the wife of Manmatha, the God of Love. The couple represented the perfect relationship in love, harmony and sexual union.

Symbolically she represents sexual passion, love, beauty and femininity. If you are searching on how to bring more passion to your relationship call Rati into your presence. Let her help you find your femininity that is so often masculinised in this modern age. Allow yourself to tap into this feminine energy to help you bring forth your desire and passion back into your relationship with your partner and yourself. Feminine energy expressed in a sensual way is a beautiful gift to yourself and to your partner. Let your inhibitions go and allow yourself to be vulnerable. Feel strength in your ability to incite passion in your partner and stay in this strength with confidence. This will be a true union of the Sensual Feminine and Powerful Masculine that combine to bring pleasure to you both and a deeper more balanced connection in your relationship.

LOST IN THE WOODS

Reilly McCarron reveals the evolution of fairy tales, and connects us to a lesser known and entrancing old Russian tale that tells of the divine feminine in her many forms…

Once upon a time every family had a storyteller. Before television and radio people told stories to each other in spinning rooms, working in the field, at the tavern, and around the hearth. There was an abundance of stories and each time one was told it changed a little to suit the setting and the audience. There are over 200 tales in the Brothers Grimm collection, yet only a handful of these are widely known. For all the fairy tales that have stood the test of time, there are many more which have slipped from our collective psyche. Even amidst the well known tales there are older, bolder versions which you will not find in a child's picture book or a Walt Disney movie. So what about all the forgotten fairy tales?

In early versions of Little Red Riding Hood the girl outwits the wolf and escapes unharmed, without the help of a passing hunter. This story, known as The Grandmother's Tale, has cannibalism, defecation, a strip tease, predatory sexuality, and a clever heroine. Charles Perrault rewrote it for the amusement of the French court in the early 17th century and in his version the wolf ate the girl - 'and let that be a lesson to you' was his point. The Brothers Grimm changed the ending so the girl was rescued, and this remains the most well known version. Many heroines have been similarly lost in the woods.

According to the renowned fairy tale academic Maria Tatar, the story of Donkeyskin was once a companion piece to Cinderella. Yet one is as unknown as the other is popular. While Cinderella's theme is maternal cruelty, Donkeyskin deals with paternal incest. Can you imagine a Disney film about a king who wishes to marry his own daughter? Fairy tales were once meant for adults. The Grimm brothers' original publication of their Nursery and Household Tales was a two-volume scholarly work but it failed to sell. Over successive editions the tales were watered down as the brothers edited them to suit an audience of children and parents. Much later, Disney continued to censor and sugar-coat a handful of tales which are among the most popular today.

So fairy tales are now widely believed to be children's stories, but if we step into the enchanted forest in search of the forgotten tales (and brave heroines amidst them) we find rich nourishment for adults. An old Russian tale, Vasalisa the Beautiful, brims with insights into the feminine. The story begins in a familiar way: a sweet young girl loses her mother and her father remarries a cruel woman with two spoilt daughters of her own. But young Vasalisa's dying mother had the foresight to gift her daughter a doll which offers protection and guidance. Unlike Cinderella, Vasalisa must embark upon a journey of courage and face Mother Death herself.

One day the wicked step-mother sent Vasalisa into the woods to meet the Baba Yaga, in an attempt to be rid of the unwanted child. Baba Yaga is an ancient witch hag who flies through the night sky in her mortar using a pestle to steer. Her hut is deep within the dark forest; it dances on chicken legs and is surrounded by a fence made from human bones and skulls that glow with an eerie light. Her cackle jangles the still air. She is both fierce and fearsome, and Vasalisa must be careful not to displease her lest the hag devour her as a tasty morsel! The girl's task is to bring home some life giving light from the terrifying crone.

This tale speaks to the divine feminine in her many forms. The good mother dies away but leaves her daughter with the gift of protection. The doll can be understood as the girl's intuition as its quiet wisdom guides her safely through a perilous initiation. The cruel mother throws the girl onto the path to womanhood. The Baba Yaga is the wild wisdom found deep within who awakes us to our potential with her frightening power. And we, like Vasalisa, must sometimes become a little lost in the woods so that we might face the many reflections of the Goddess in ourselves.

Reilly McCarron is the creator and enchantress of 'faerie bard', and President of the Australian Fairy Tale Society. She is a singer/songwriter, a Bard with the Order of Bards, Ovates and Druids (OBOD), an accredited member of the Australian Storytelling Guild (NSW) and has a Graduate Diploma in Australian Folklore with a particular interest in fairy tales. Contact Reilly at: Email: austfairytales@gmail.com Web: www.facebook.com/austfairytales

Artwork Credit – Regan Kubecek www.facebook.

Mother Tara - Feminine Ideal in Buddhist Tradition

By Radnamaya

Goddess Tara - Female Buddha and Meditation Tantra:

She is considered to be the goddess of Universal compassion who represents virtuous and enlightened activity. Her compassion for living beings, her desire to save them from suffering, is said to be even stronger than a mothers' love for her children.

The story of Tara's origin, according to the Tara Tantra, recounts that aeons ago she was born as a king's daughter. A spiritual and compassionate princess, she regularly gave offerings and prayers to the ordained monks and nuns. She thus developed great merit, and the monks told her that, because of her spiritual attainment, they would pray that she be reborn as a man and spread Buddhist teachings.

She responded that there was no male and no female, that nothing existed in reality, and that she wished to remain in female form to serve other beings until everyone reached Enlightenment, hence implying the shortfall in the monk's knowledge in presuming only male preachers for the Buddhist Tradition.

Thus Tara might be considered one of the earliest feminists.

Another legend of Tara is that she was born from the compassionate tears of Avalokiteshvara (The Buddha of Compassion).

On a lotus seat, standing for realization of voidness,

(You are) the emerald – coloured, one faced, two armed lady.

In youth's full bloom, right leg out, left drawn in,

Showing the union of wisdom and art – Homage to you!

Like the out stretched branch of the heavenly turquoise tree,

Your supple right hand makes the boon – granting gesture,

Inviting the wise to a feast of supreme accomplishments,

As if to an entertainment – Homage to you!

Your left hand gives us refuge,

Showing the three jewels,

It says " You people who see a hundred dangers, Don't be frightened, I shall swiftly save you" – Homage to you!

Both hands signal with blue Utpala flowers,

"Samsaric beings! Cling not to worldly pleasures.

Enter the great city of liberation!"

Flower – goads prodding us to effort – Homage to you!

First Dalai Lama (1391 – 1474)

Words inspired by my Guru from Radnamaya.
You can contact Radnamaya by email: radnamaya@live.com

For the love of Angels

By Suzanne Hartas

LIKE THE SEED THAT IS BURIED BENEATH THE SOIL AND RISES TO THE SURFACE TO BE ONE WITH THE LIGHT, SO TOO, YOUR SPIRIT IS RISING TO BE ONE WITH THE LIGHT.

The Angels say "My Dear Ones, it is our honor to support you in these blessed times of transformation and renewal upon your Earth. For you see, you have chosen to incarnate at a time when your planet is in much need of restoration and healing and you have bravely elected to play an instrumental role in the rebirthing of your new world.

The Divine Feminine energy is arising from within you and is igniting the flame of desire for the remembrance of the truth of your divinity. It is in the light of the Oneness, is where you will find the peace, harmony and balance for which you seek my Beloved Ones.

Many would believe this sacred energy has long been suppressed and denied, however, as you well know, all is divinely orchestrated and the resurgence of her energy at this time is in accordance with the Creators plan. For the Creator has awaited your readiness and willingness to embrace this arising energy and recognize that you have indeed always held this power within.

As you delve deeply within and merge once again with the completeness of your spirit, the veil of your God self will be lifted and just as the flowers beauty rises to meet the sun, so too will your spirit rise to greet the light of God. Surrender to the Divine Feminine within and allow her voice of wisdom to speak through you, her heart of love to radiate from you and her dance of freedom to flow through you. May her strength and courage hold you steady as you ascend and merge into the absolute completeness of LOVE. The doorway between heaven and earth is becoming increasingly transparent and your world will reflect only Heaven's Love. Love is God and you are Love. Blessed times are upon you now. Many blessings and much love Beloved Ones

Susanne Hartas is a Psychic Medium and Angel Intuitive.

Please contact Suzanne at:
www.inspiritmagazine.com
mail@inspiritmagazine.com

SOUL LOVE
IN MODERN DAY

Amanda Roussety gives us something to think about here about what it is we need to create the deep Soul Love we all desire.

Relationships are becoming disposable and people perceive it easier to let go of love than to let go of stress. We spend our single days searching for the right person, the one to complete us and fill a lonely void, but when we finally find it, do we really know what to do with it?

How is it that so many in our grandparents' generation stayed together through thick and through thin? It's not as if they lived lives without stress and worry, but they somehow managed to pull together and find the meaning of what being a couple is all about.

We are in the social media era, which means that the way we communicate is very different from previous generations. People are detached from their true emotions and this only results in empty, unfulfilled relationships. Do we want that? NO! Of course not, but in a modern society of detached love, how does one reconnect to our inherent desire to be connected completely from the depth of our soul to another? I see it almost daily in my office at Infinite Soul in Narellan. Many of my clients are detached from their true emotions and they feel so lost as they search for something greater in the area of personal relationships but have no idea what that really is.

As a romantic female I know all too well the unrealistic expectations we create from online quotes, pictures and watching movies. Mr Right is sensitive, but masculine; he can build you a home with his bare hands, while cooking you dinner and cleaning at the same time. He is adventurous and a deep thinker but loves to interact with you and listen to your thoughts and feelings. This sensual man knows passion and even though he may have been hurt, all he needs to do is meet you and the rest will be perfect.

Sounds like the perfect plan right? But in a world filled with bumps and curves how can our 'perfect plan' ever really have a smooth journey?

And I'm sorry to burst your bubble ladies, but you too have baggage that can interrupt the smooth sailing. I've always said there is perfection in imperfection, and in relationships this couldn't be truer. Finding each other's imperfections and learning to love each one with a passion so consuming that sometimes it hurts, that's love. Really seeing this person who has been hurt, the same person who is capable of hurting you, that one, crazy, yet amazing person who mirrors your own fears and insecurities, and makes you face your own demons. That's perfect soul love.

So what is it that people want?

That is debatable I guess, and I can not speak for everyone especially the men whose desires are still a bit foggy even to me.

I have asked numerous women what they really want from a man and there is a common theme being expressed time and time again. Ultimately the majority of women want a man who is simply 'a man', the essence of man in his entirety. Yes it really is that simple. The issue woman face is that we are generally quite 'full-on' creatures. As the holders of the womb and all the inherent nurturing that comes with that, we carry heavily on our shoulders the burdens of our loved ones, our careers, our friends and anyone else we come across. This overload of emotion can often leave a woman feeling unbalanced and scattered. Masculine energy helps the feminine to balance and ground their scattered energy so that they can focus on priorities in their life.

So in a modern society that leaves us struggling to openly connect, how do we connect to and then express these inherent desires?

Well, let's begin by having a little look at dating. So many these days find relationships via online dating sites, only to discover that the passion and level of open communication displayed by their online romantic interest disappears the moment verbal communication replaces their computer screens. I hear so many stories from my female friends on how they had all these expectations only to end up disappointed and deflated by the whole process. But the key message I hear from those that have had online dating success, is that they had no expectations and were open to whatever came their way. Because of this lack of a 'fairy tale' expectation created from modern society, each person was happy to speak their truth and stand proudly in their truth. This helped them to be honest about who they are and what they really want in their life.

We humans need to not only learn how to bring forth our truth but learn again how to communicate these needs so that our lover can understand us with clarity.

We women must learn to embrace our inner goddess, our divine feminine power, and we must allow who we truly are to flow in the rhythm of life.

So who is this goddess, and what does her feminine power enable her to do? She is compassionate, but strong, powerful yet delicate. This goddess's greatest gift to man is her ability to provide pure

compassionate love. A love that nurtures like a mother nurtures a new born baby, delicately and unconditionally. A love that shows support and strength, more powerful than the strongest earthly metals.

Men really are from a different planet to women and we need to see this as a beautiful thing, not something that forges resistance within us. Understanding our beautiful men for what they bring to us and our world is one of the key ways to help the true feminine emerge.

Yes, he may have been wounded by his past and maybe even wounded multiple times leaving scars that may never fully heal, but you need to look at his scars with love, seeing them for the strength they have created with in him that now flows outwardly into this hostile world. Look into these old wounds knowing that even though the scars will never completely disappear, they will fade, becoming only a fleeting reminder of the journey, and the impact they once had will eventually become a distant memory.

And when he hurts you with his sharp fiery tongue, see the scared child who is reacting to their inner pain and their inner fears, see that little boy who has lost the way of heart feeling through detached emotion. Do not react from a place of inner fear, for this will only separate you more, but instead stand in your strength, assert your truth without childhood name calling and angered words.

You too may have wounds that hurt still and the best thing you can do is love and nurture yourself, accepting your own journey, but do not hold onto the pain. Instead, see the beautiful vibrant flower that you have emerged as now coming into bloom and allow the masculine energy of your man to do its job, providing you with the strong foundation needed for this healing to take place.

Accept your man and remember the power of the feminine is far greater than any other power on earth - the same power that creates and holds the future of the human race within its own womb, the same power that nurtures from its breast the most abundant and pure love through the heart chakra.

This is why almost every man on the planet desires the closeness of a woman's breast, because whether they realise it or not, it brings a deep pure love and nurturing that the masculine energy needs for its own balance. The masculine spends so much time being 'man', being strength and protection to so many. As a son, brother, mate, husband and then father, their role is relentless and, like women, it is called on and demanded constantly.

So what is the true message here? What is it that we need to create this deep soul love that is desired by so many? We simply need to be love, to give love and be open to receiving love. When we do this wholeheartedly we begin to see each other with clarity and acceptance. For neither of us are without flaws, but if perfection is found in imperfection, then maybe the perfection we seek has been under our noses the whole time.

Amanda Roussety is a Celebrity Psychic Medium & Spiritual development Teacher. Accomplishments include becoming a finalist on channel sevens 'The One' and being the NSW Psychic of the Year 2013. Amanda is the cofounder of Infinite Soul Spiritual development centre in Narellan, NSW. For more information go to www.infinitesoul.com.au or www.amandaroussety.com

Sacred, Sensual, Sexy
~The Feminine Power Within~

Gem leads the way for you to awaken and accept the Divine Essence within, and better still how to bottle this essence to use whenever you want to honour this sacredness we all have within ourselves...

Oh the Feminine Divine! The goddess in all her glory. The sacredness of our bodies and the divine beauty within. The sensuality and sexiness of feminine divinity, oh my! Such beautiful creatures are these feminine beings, so powerful in their skin. The depths of the sacred energy is a never ending water way, changing, evolving, flowing, yet always, always sacred.

Long forgotten is the sacred and divine feminine beauty that we each as powerful women hold within our sacred self's. A lifetime of limited thought and media influence has ensured that we believe we are less than if we are not what 'they' say we should be or should look like.

Plastered with all kinds of media depicting and brain washing us to believe that everything we are is on the surface. Misdirected so that we don't delve deep and discover the true beauty and power within our bellies, our wombs and our souls.

Guess what though goddesses? It is not about how we look! Our own sacred, sensual, sexy comes from how we feel which in turn comes from what we believe. Our sacred feminine divinity comes from within. Our sensual, sexy inner goddess is just that, on the inside!

The key to releasing our inner goddess and raising her to the surface is belief! It is a belief that we have in ourselves, in our own divine feminine energy. This belief in ourselves creates the confidence to allow us to sit in our own unique femininity and to accept all women for theirs.

Allowing ourselves to accept and honour our own feminine divinity comes from a deep, honest belief in who we are. Creating and living with that feeling, that inner knowing, that belief that we are sacred and sensual goddesses each as unique and amazing as the next begins with giving ourselves permission to feel it deep inside. It also means ignoring ALL who tell you otherwise. If you believe it, it is true. It is your truth.

Oshun, Divine Goddess of Sensuality, shared visions with me of worlds long forgotten where women were held most sacred with a focus on the all-encompassing love; pure love, pure compassion, pure insight, pure foresight, pure wisdom. She calls for us to raise our awareness of the power of our own sacred femininity. It is time to rejoice in our bodies and to rejoice in our minds. It is time to revel in all that makes our hearts sing and it is time to do it for ourselves.

As we awaken ourselves, as more and more women discover and celebrate their divine feminine self's openly and confidently, we begin to allow our sisters, our mothers, our daughters, our aunts and our nieces, the freedom to discover and rejoice in their sacred self's too.

We begin to allow our beautiful boys, brothers, fathers and uncles too, to see the magnificent sorcery and sacredness of womanhood, the sacredness and divine power that the feminine psyche holds and we begin to re-teach them the ways to honour and respect ALL women.

By regaining respect for and honouring ourselves, by rejoicing in our true authentic feminine selves, we create a ripple effect thus creating a difference for generations to come.

Sacred Sensual Connections

Gather:

Fresh Flower petals of your choosing

Bath Oil or Salts ~ Rose Scented would be nice

Candles ~ Red, Natural, Green or Pink (one or all)

Glass Jar or Vessel

Draw a bath filled with bubbles and scents of your choosing. Place your candles around the bathtub and room. As you light them, call in the divine spirit or the goddess – Oshun, Amphitrite, Yemaya - and state your intent to discover and trust in your sacred sensual self.

Take one flower petal and toss it into your sacred bath as you acknowledge something fabulous that you like or love about yourself such as 'I am beautiful', 'I am smart', 'I love my eyes', 'I love my fingers'...

When there is nothing else positive you can acknowledge about yourself, slip into the bath and immerse yourself. Soak in your goddess essence. Nourish your soul with your sensuality and nurture your body with your divine sexiness.

When you know, accept, trust and believe in your own feminine power, remove yourself, gather your petals, place them in your glass jar or vessel, add some of your bath water and a little vodka for preservation. Keep your personal Feminine Divine Essence to remind you of your sacred sensual being, use on altars, place in your bedroom or sacred space or add a splash to future baths.

Gem~mer is an Ocean Enchantress, Intuitive Creatress and Teacher of Ocean Magicks. Gem's creative works include crafting ocean talismans and tools for spiritual connections and teaching ocean magicks through magazine articles, workshops and online courses. Gem~mer has also begun the magickal journey of creating oracle and insight decks, books and birthing illuminating retreats as a way of sharing and teaching the magick and wisdom of ocean and sea's. 'May the Wisdom and Magick of Ocean and Sea's Inspire Us All'. www.cryshellmagic.com.au

Sacred Snake Shifting

Embracing the teachings of the Serpent and recent Snake Year, Natasha Heard shares how to work with the power of sacred Snake Magick to release fear and shed all that is unwanted, to emerge into this world with a renewed sense of Self and Purpose…

2013 was the Chinese Year of the Snake. I could feel the energy of that year so strongly, it was a tough year for most, a year to shed our skins and grow beyond our limits. Most people I knew, including myself, were going through rapid growth and the only way to move forward was to release what we no longer needed in our lives, to shed our skins.

By the end of that year I could literally feel the last few scales falling away, I was free of the tight bonds that held me back and I was ready to leap into the future full of new energy! In this year of the Snake I also found myself the guardian of two beautiful pythons who have been creature teachers to me, silently imparting their wisdom upon me in many ways.

The Serpent is a sensual being, it slides and slinks and connects straight to a woman's sense of self-confidence, her sensual self, her sexual nature. If you are afraid of your own sensual self, your own power, your inner goddess; be her calm and beautiful or raging and wild, getting over your fear of Snake and connecting with her can help you immensely. A snake can bite yes, this is true and with my own experience with my pythons they will only strike if you are not centred, grounded and moving at a snakes pace. This means time spent with my pythons is in the moment, I must forget all the 'I have to do's' and appointments for tomorrow, I must simply breath and be present in that moment, moving slowly and knowing my own power and the power of the Snake.

I have noticed so many people are very fearful of snakes and I am very proud to say I have seen the hate transform into, not love but at least acceptance, respect and like right before my eyes. I have seen trembling hands become calm under the sliding belly of placid snake. They actually give out the energy of calmness.

If holding a real snake is too much for you, perhaps you can simply visualise what it would be like to actually be a snake. Imagine your body shapeshifting into that of a single channel, a body long and slender, without skin but with silken scales sliding from left to right out in the wilderness, lifting your head above the grass to see into the distance, flicking your tongue to smell the air. Feel your grounded, centred spirit, feel your power, your inner spark of divinity growing. You have gained so much new wisdom, you have allowed yourself to become more than you ever have before and now your outer skin begins to feel tight. You want so desperately to feel free of this bondage so you begin to rub your face against a soft mossy rock before you and you break open the dead outer layer to reveal not a scale but soft new skin, your own face is revealed, vibrant and beautiful, your bright aura shines through this crack like a ray of sunlight and you begin to wipe away the old skin revealing more and more beautiful skin, hair, shoulders, elbows… Take your time, move with snakes pace, there is no rush. Feel that with each push out of this skin you are leaving behind all that has burdened you, all that has kept you from living your dreams is shed away with this dead skin. When you are ready you stand. You are beautiful, you are grounded and centred and you are glowing with your own inner power.

Thank the Sensual Serpent for allowing you to merge with the great energy of Snake and watch out world - now nothing can hold you back!

Natasha Heard is a creatress of all things magical! A natural witch ~ her magical life and connection to the Earth flow into all her creations. Specialising in Wands, Sceptres and Staves; and creating with her horticulturalist husband Michael, Blessed Rune sets and Tree of Life Bind Rune Talismans. Her innate connection with all aspects of the natural world and passion for magic is what makes her a true creatress of powerful, magical tools. Natasha can be contacted at: www.blessedbranches.com Email: blessedbranches@gmail.com or flowerlove@live.com.au / Facebook: Blessed Branches…magical tools by Natasha Heard. Artwork Credit - Nicolle Poll www.facebook.com/ArtworkByNicolle

Love Between the Lines

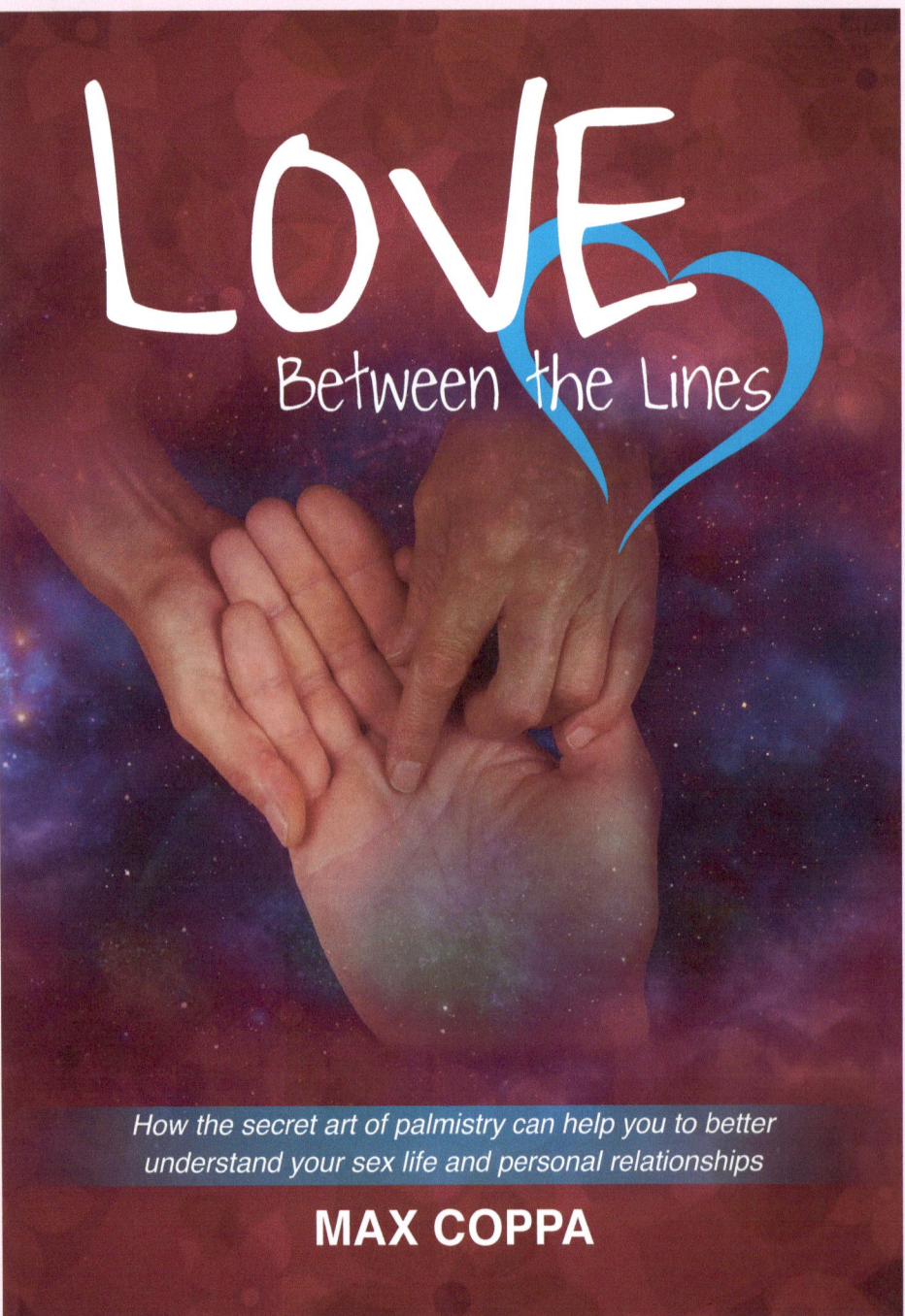

How the secret art of palmistry can help you to better understand your sex life and personal relationships

MAX COPPA

By Max Coppa

An extract from Love Between the Lines: How the secret art of palmistry can help you to better understand your sex life and personal relationships.

published by inSpirit Publishing)

The hands have it!

Throughout the ages, humans have looked at their palms to provide answers almost in the way that today we might look at a roadmap for direction. In a sense, your palm is actually a blueprint for your life's journey. Understanding this blueprint enables you to access information not only about future trends but also about a whole range of 'here' and 'now' issues such as relationships, health, work, money and travel. Looking at the palm, first take note of the size and shape of the hands, the mounts, the lines on the mounts and the lines interlacing the palm. For right-handed people, the left hand reflects inbred characteristics and the right hand acquired characteristics. The opposite is true for left-handed people. Each mount signifies a certain personality trait with the four most important lines representing life, intelligence, the heart and personal fortune. Also important are the size and shape of the fingers and the fingertips.

Your hands show you the spiritual and physical directions that lie before you. Although you ultimately determine your own destiny, at times we all need a little glimpse

To visit Max: www.maxcoppa.com Facebook: www.facebook.com/maxcoppapsychic
Love Between the Lines is available for presale soon.

Your hands show you the spiritual and physical directions that lie before you.

of the road ahead in order to give our lives meaning and purpose. Past events and conditions have conspired to make you what you are today while the present holds the seeds of opportunity for shaping the future. Palmistry can help illuminate past weaknesses or strengths, the knowledge of which can empower you to steer a wiser course for that future. At first trying to read a palm may appear to be a little overwhelming. The key is to take it step by step and remember to have fun while you're learning – and soon you'll be well on the way to understanding the secrets of your own and your lover's palm.

One of the most important things to remember when you begin to analyse anyone's hands (including those of your partner) is to always read both hands. Most people have a dominant hand, meaning they are either right-handed or left-handed and the dominant and non-dominant hands have different meanings.

The non-dominant or passive hand; (the one you don't use to write with) shows your basic personality, natural aptitudes, characteristics, past and current events and inner life, as well as your innate potential. It is the reflection of the innermost you.

The dominant hand; (the one you do use to write with) shows how your personality has changed or is likely to develop. It indicates future events as well as what you are doing with your life right now.

Very often, the hands reveal marked differences between our innate potential and the degree to which it is being fulfilled.

Size

The first thing you'll notice about your own or your lover's hands is the size. Most people have roughly the same sized hands, although women's hands are marginally smaller, in general, than those of men. From time to time though, you'll no doubt encounter people whose hand size is at the extreme of both ends of the scale.

Small Hands: Contrary to what you might expect, a person whose hands are small is intensely interested in the grand scheme of things. They see life on a big scale. Fiercely ambitious with visions of grandeur when it comes to lifestyle, they like big houses, big cars and always have an eye on the main chance. As lovers though, they can be nitpickers who may drive you crazy with their nagging. They tend to like drama and are drawn to the erotic and purely physical side of sex. Often guided by pure intuition, they tend to be more emotional than mental. In love, they are risk-takers who love living through the senses.

Large Hands: These are the hands of an attentive lover. If these are your hands, you look at life in great detail, particularly when it comes to relationships. You're the sort who will ponder long and hard before making a commitment, but once you've run the idea through that analytical computer brain of yours and the data has come up looking good, you're very user-friendly – and loyal. Your powers of concentration and memory are legendary, so any partner should be forewarned against trying to pull the wool over your eyes with stories about exactly where they were and with whom on the night of the 14th eight months ago!

Thickness

Thickness of the hand is also a very good indicator of exactly how much sexual energy we have at our disposal. To check the hand for thickness, view it from the side. Take note, though, that other factors, such as the size of the Mount of Venus and the depth of the lines (more on this later), can modify what a thickness reading can tell you. Remember the rule in palmistry is to take everything in the hand into account.

Thin Hands: A person with thin hands is often lacking in true warmth of the heart, a quality vital to a really deep and lasting relationship. This is especially true if the hand is hard as well as thin, indicating stubbornness, inflexibility, reserve and a somewhat secretive, calculating approach. They may not always be 100 per cent truthful, and they can also be real misers when it comes to spending money in a relationship.

Thick Hands: Here we find the complete opposite to be true. A thick hand reveals an abundance of warm energy and sensuality. If the hand is thick and soft as well, they'll love sex and especially food, and may have difficulty maintaining a balanced weight. A thick hand that is also hard and inflexible usually indicates someone who is sexually aggressive as well as emotionally demanding, thinking mostly about self-gratification. This person would prove very difficult to live with, as basically there is too much take and not enough give.

Max Coppa is Australia's leading expert in Palmistry, Numerology & Dream Interpretation with over 35 years experience. With an extensive background in media, Max has appeared on national television & radio, has contributed to many leading Australian magazines and is the published author of four books. Max writes a regular column for That's Life Magazine and appears on Channel 7's The Morning Show and PsychicTV. Max's inspiring and practical approach brings palmistry and numerology in to the 21st century and makes it accessible to all. Max has a passion for teaching others and conducts palmistry & numerology workshops throughout Australia.

The Sacred Seamstress

As Kye Crowe cuts, stitches and embellishes her sacred gowns – a beautiful and unique kind of magic is being energetically woven into these stunning creations that celebrate the Divine Goddess within…

For almost thirty years I have been creating clothing that celebrates the Goddess and helps women connect with their own Divine beauty.

I have seen many women feeling run down and battered from their lives emerge from my changing room looking so radiant and beautiful in one of my Goddess dresses, they were astounded when they looked in the mirror and saw their own gorgeous reflection.

I know that beautiful clothes can help us connect with our own inner beauty and bring it out, but over my years of creating as a Sacred Seamstress I know that how the clothes are created is of vital importance too.

In the same way that we can open people's hearts when we prepare a meal in a space of love, the way our clothing is made can have a similar impact. In fact everything we use in our lives has a vibration and energetically affects us.

When we wear clothing that was created with integrity, honouring our earth and all beings involved in the process, it vibrates those qualities and we can feel uplifted simply from wearing it. And when our clothing is created in a sacred space it doesn't only enhance our own sense of wellbeing, it is a tool that helps us connect with our own magical self.

Whenever I sew now I see myself as a sacred chalice overflowing with the Divine. Very often I will purify my space before I begin and will smudge myself with herbs. If I need to access some extra energy I will play my wooden shaman sticks or beat my drum as I walk around my workshop, charging it with vibrant energy. If I am feeling tight in my body I will put on some music and dance or do some yogic stretching. It is always important I let go of stress or anything that will distract me from being totally present to my creative process.

When I feel I'm ready to begin, I light a candle that burns brightly as I work and symbolises my connection with the Goddess and the person I am creating for.

Most times I don't know and haven't yet connected physically with the person that will eventually buy or receive my creation but I hear the whispers of spirit as I work and on one occasion they said to me "She needs more Mother Earth energy around her belly and place a prayer mandala over her heart with some rose quartz crystal sewn in".

When I finally met the Goddess this cape had been created for she was in grief at losing her stillborn babe. My cape would never take that pain away but as I wrapped it around her shoulders I knew it would give her strength in her darkness and when the time was right, like a tiny little crocus bursting through the snow, remind her that spring always follows winter and in Spring everything is reborn.

I have let go of self-doubt about whom I am being guided to create for. I am awed by this process when I do. I intuitively gather fabrics together with no idea if I am about to make an ephemeral dress, a Goddess gown or an elven tunic. I simply let go to the flow. It's like a dance and I only trip and fall if I let my head get involved in the process and question what I'm feeling intuitively guided to create.

Oh there are times when I lose the flow completely and fail to see anything beautiful emerging from the process, but that's ok. It happens, we get distracted but we can always reconnect. If I take some deep breaths and sigh out any doubt or go for a walk or sit under a tree, I soon feel the inspiration calling me once again.

Over the years I have created for Goddesses of all shapes and sizes and ages and most of them wished they were either slimmer or taller or younger. As I stitch and embellish my sacred gowns the mantra I hear most of all is 'I Accept'.

It may not seem like the most magical mantra, but if women were to accept that their own beauty was not dependent on the shallowness of age or weight or the size of their hips, but in the depth that they feel and give and love, a new consciousness of compassion and love would be birthed on our earth, as the Goddess in us all awakens.

Kye Crow is the Creatress of Wunjo Crow, a range of Goddess clothing that's sprinkled with love and sewn with magic. Kye and her partner Gill live with over a 100 rescued animals and teach Sacred Journeys into the Animal Realms, the power of Love and how to live on planet earth as a sensitive.
Contact Kye at: Web: www.camelcampsanctuary.com / Facebook: www.facebook.com/Wunjocrow
Photo Credit: Argnesh Rose Visionary Digital Artist specialising in fantasy and totem portraiture – www.givethemwings.com.au

Cosmic Codes
with Amanda Coppa

Moon Magic for the months ahead.

JULY 2014

9:25pm AEST Saturday 12

The full moon in the earthy and responsible sign of Capricorn brings tests, karmic patterns and growth challenges to the surface. It's an opportune time to take stock of our experiences and master our lessons. We must understand that everything we do, say or think directly affects ourselves and others. Irrespective of our situation we each have choices to make, and as we assume responsibility for the vital part we play in the stage show of life, we begin to flow more easily. Use this time to expand your perceptions and go beyond your limitations. **Tip for Capricorns:** Don't allow personal issues to detract you from what you need to do.

8:42am AEST Sunday 27

The new moon in the vibrant and dynamic sign of Leo ushers in a new wave of inspired energy. It's time to align with your purpose and courageously follow your dreams without delay. Now is the perfect time to create, enhance or awaken your natural creativity, passion and vitality. Creative hobbies such as art, music, design or writing are especially enhanced now. Let your light shine brightly for all to see and back yourself as you unashamedly live the life you are meant to.

Tip for Leos: Believe in what you are doing and stick to your guns.

AUGUST 2014

4:10am AEST Monday 11

The full moon in the innovative and visionary sign of Aquarius brings much insight and awareness in to our consciousness. The symbol of Aquarius is the water bearer who shares wisdom and knowledge freely and equally to all. This moon fans our inner flame and reminds us to be open and receptive to all of life's wisdom. Some lessons we learn easily, while others will leave scars as a reminder of a valuable lesson learned. The keyword for Aquarius is 'I know' and we are encouraged now to detach from drama and be true to ourselves. We know what to do, we just need to do it! **Tip for Aquarians:** Now is the time to learn then share your knowledge with others.

12:13am AEST Tuesday 26

Cleansing and purification is the theme of the new moon in the health conscious sign of Virgo. The new moon marks a time of self-awareness, healing and renewal for us all. Has your life or personal environment become energetically toxic? The energy of Virgo encourages us to review the way we are currently doing, or are perceiving things in our life and make necessary changes to perfect it. You may be guided to exercise, improve your diet or simply rest more under the new moon. Whatever it is, take positive action when guided and watch your situation improve.

Tip for Virgos: Avoid falling in to old patterns. Now is the time to clear the blocks.

SEPTEMBER 2014

11:38am AEST Tuesday 9

The full moon in the deep and receptive sign of Pisces beckons us to peel back our layers and awaken our Spirit. Pisces is deeply connected to feelings, senses and mysticism, yet it can be very impressionable and prone to illusion. The full moon illuminates the importance of exploring our emotions and truly feeling our experiences through our heart. Using our five senses to be fully present and really connect in the now moment brings us alive. A wave of new-found clarity, peace and contentment is here for us now. We only need to release our resistance, see the truth beyond the illusion and honor the calling of our Soul. **Tip for Pisceans:** Keep your feet on the ground and be honest with yourself.

4:14pm AEST Wednesday 24

Emotional healing, balance and renewal is the key theme of the new moon in the peace-loving sign of Libra. Our relationships with others, how we give and receive love, including our capacity to love and honour ourselves, is highlighted. Now is the time to restore balance in our daily lives and tap into the deepest sources of spiritual wisdom and healing. As we work on healing and accepting ourselves we naturally create pathways for others to do the same.

Tip for Librans: Love who you are and don't settle for anything less than you deserve.

Amanda Coppa is a heart-centred crystal healer who incorporates astrology, numerology, Reiki and oracle cards into her work. She is passionate about self-healing, empowerment and helping you understand the REAL you.

Connect with Amanda at http://www.facebook.com/cosmiccodes.

Rita Maher delves into the world of young hearts and as the adults in their world, how important and formative the care of their hearts you offer can be…

Nurturing Puppy Love

Puppy love, one's first crush, the first flutter of butterflies as that special person walks by in the school yard. We have all been there, all experienced it and all have tale to tell.

Remember back to when you first felt giddy how old where you? And more importantly did you talk to your parents about it. Chances are if you did they dismissed it as 'puppy love' or thought 'how cute your first crush' or maybe even pumped you up about how popular you are and how you had them all chasing you. Perhaps you were too afraid to even mention it and especially not at the dinner table were siblings could run with this information and create mileage with teasing taunts and singing about who you were caught kissing in a tree.

No matter if it's at preschool, kindergarten, primary or the first years of high school, one's first love can leave a lasting impression on your child's life. The way that it is viewed by their peers, by you as parents and the social world around them can have an impact on how they handle this first foray into a life time of exploring emotions.

The start of a child's school life can be a daunting process, finding how they fit in a new environment challenges everyone. The playground becomes the scene of many first loves and can set in motion the way our children view themselves at times. The child with the harem of others vying for their attention is sure to feel confident and can even be a little cocky at times. Strutting their stuff through the playground with admiring glances from all attracted to this show of self-worth. While the child who lustful feelings are rejected by their interest can be made to feel inadequate, even cast aside in the jostling for social standing, never understanding why they were rejected.

In later years school dances, discos become the scene while all the boys and girls dance in groups there is always some who want to dance with each other but how is going to ask who? What if they are rejected or teased and how will it be viewed by their social circle. Perhaps there is even pressure for all to have a partner or not be part of the group at all. Young hearts can be crushed before even leaving the starting gate.

Enter in the high school years and hormones come in play havoc, our children's self-worth, emotions and sanity is tested here. Intense whirl winds of emotions flow through our teenager's veins, often unexplainable to themselves let alone to you. Except now not only does this play out in the school it plays out in social media circles. Mobile phones, Facebook, Kik, all allow for news to spread quickly and without thought. Your teenager can get hundreds of 'likes' or 'attacks' depending on how they are viewed all of which affect their self-worth and brings their emotions into question. Now puppy love or one's first crush becomes fair game for all to comment on and for all to put pressure on.

Our response to all this is important. How we listen, understand, empathise and advise our children as they walk through the stages of exploring emotions of love, *admiration, lust and rejection will shape the way they handle future experience in life. They are young and care free, their hearts are unbroken and as parents we want them to stay that way, yet from our own experiences we know that there will be hurts, tears and questions of why.*

The trick here is not to wrap them in cotton wool, life happens. They need to be able to deal with love and loss and become resilient, understanding well-adjusted individuals. If we nurture them and show that they will always be loved by family and to love themselves, ensuring them that there is nothing wrong with them and they don't need to change who they are to be loved; then this process of exploring young love will be more joyous. They will be able to share with you wonderful tales of their first kiss, secret notes passed in class, that first dance and first date. In return for your nurturing you get the joy of watching them grow and become beautiful souls both inside and out as they walk through life not fearing love and emotion, rather embracing it for all its beauty.

Rita Maher is a Psychic Medium, Intuitive Counsellor and qualified Reiki Healer who has a passion for working with children and families. She specialises in meditation and intuitive guidance to help not just children but adults understand direction and change in their life, helping create secure environments for young minds to grow and thrive.

Mystic Elixir for LOVE

Meadow Linn entices us with scentualities of food...

There are many paths to enlightenment and many routes to a fulfilling, happy, and harmonious life. However, simply by cooking and eating with intention and mindfulness, you can elevate your consciousness and enhance your life.

Cook up some magic today and enter into the mystical world of the ancient alchemists. A dash of imagination, a sprinkle of intuition, and an ounce of intention, and your kitchen will be filled with potent energy and delicious treats to savor.

Grab your magic apron, and away we go!

With a small pot, a handful of mystic ingredients, and an open and accepting heart, you can call forth powerful love alchemy into your life. Spice up the love in your life. Enhance your connection to yourself, your sweetie, and your family and friends with this delicious mystic elixir. Here's to creating potent kitchen alchemy!

A little history about these magical ingredients:

MYSTIC CHOCOLATE:

Drink mystic chocolate and tap into the wisdom of the ancient Maya who so revered cacao that they consumed it in large quantities and believed it was also a favorite of the gods. The scientific name of the cacao tree (Theobroma cacao) means "food of the gods." The cacao was ground into a paste and mixed with honey, maize, and chili to make a frothy beverage thought to have many sacred powers. According to legend, Montezuma drank 50 cups a day to enhance his virility. What magic can you cook up with some cocoa?

MYSTIC HONEY:

Make your life sweeter with a few drops of mystic honey! Throughout history, honey has symbolized all that is sweet in life. In many traditions, it was believed honey made the gods immortal. And bees have been revered as intermediaries between heaven, earth, and the underworld. Honey is also sacred in many cultures because of its many healing properties. Grab your Honey and share some mystic cocoa sweetened with the intoxicating energy of honey.

MYSTIC CHILIES:

Sprinkle ground chilies into your cocoa with the deliberate intention to fire up the love in your life, and you'll be on your way to learning one of the alchemical secrets of a Mystic Chef®. Additionally, many cultures around the world consider chili peppers to be an aphrodisiac. The color red stimulates dynamic energy and vigor. Passion, sensuality, and sexuality are also closely associated with red. And capsaicin releases endorphins, which gives us a natural high.

RECIPE:

- Serves 2
- 3 cups whole milk or favorite non-dairy milk*
- 1/2 cup unsweetened cocoa powder
- Pinch of salt
- 1/4 cup honey
- 1 or 2 sprinkles of cayenne pepper

(*Some non-dairy milks will curdle a bit, but the cocoa will still be delicious)

Whisk the milk, cocoa powder, and salt together in a small pan over medium heat. Add the honey and stir to combine. Sprinkle in the cayenne pepper with intention and mix thoroughly. Continue to heat until steaming and frothy (but not boiling), whisking frequently

As you whisk the cocoa, you're bringing energy and vitality to your love life. As you drizzle the honey, you're imbuing your life with sweetness. With each pinch of chili, you're adding spice and zest to your love life and calling forth passion for both self and others.

As you stir, repeat this affirmation: "My life is filled with love. I am loving and I am loved." As you drink this magic elixir, repeat the affirmation again. Love will begin to flood your life in the most wondrous and unexpected ways!

Enjoy by yourself or with your special Honey.

Meadow Linn is a writer and a chef, living in California with her dog, cats and chicken. She believes that living well and eating well should be tasty and fun. Meadow has just co-authored her first cookbook with Denise Linn which is available now through Amazon. **Contact Meadow at**: www.meadowlinn.com and www.savortheday.com

The Power of Intuition in the Workplace

By Simone Milasas

Imagine being at work, going through your day and accomplishing the tasks that are assigned to you with a sense of ease, with a sense of joy and even with a sense of fun and playfulness. Would that be different from your current experience? Is that something you would like to have more of?

There is this intangible and yet powerful thing called intuition that dynamically contributes to creating the life you desire in every area including your body, your career and your relationships. Incorporating intuition into your daily work experience can literally transform your workplace.

So what is intuition? According to the Webster dictionary, intuition is the ability to know something immediately without the need for reasoning. In a word or two, intuition is knowing; it's awareness.

From the time we are small, we are taught to function from logic and reasoning. We make decisions and solve problems from our mind. We gather the data, review the information and then determine the best course of action based upon the "facts". In reality, this is can be very limiting. The mind can only confirm what it already knows.

Awareness however, goes beyond the mind. It's a knowing that's far greater than the limited capacities we tend to function in. It's the space of possibilities that we have not yet considered and when you rely on your knowing, your awareness, your intuition, you begin to create an entirely different reality than the one you're currently in.

Accessing your Awareness

No matter what your background is, no matter where you have come from, we all have the ability to know things without the need for reasoning. It's something we are born with. Because intuition is often minimized and viewed as inferior to intellect, many of us have done what we can to turn off our awareness so as to fit in. The good news is your awareness is still there. It never goes away.

Here are a few tools to assist with accessing your awareness so that you can create the reality that you would like to have - even in the workplace.

1. Ask Questions

According to Gary Douglas, founder of Access Consciousness, questions open the door to all possibilities. Question are key in taking you past the confines of your limited understanding and into the space of knowing.

When you are at work, and you encounter a situation that is challenging, whether it be a difficult co-worker, an unhappy customer or an important business decision, ask questions. You can ask "What else is possible here that I haven't considered?" "What's it going to take to change this?" "What could I do different in this situation in order to create a new reality?" "How does it get any better than this?"

When you ask questions you will have an awareness of what to do next. Follow your knowing and watch things change as if by magic.

2. Trust your Knowing

Our society functions on the premise that the experts know best. When it comes to business, relationships, money, any topic you can think of, the common idea is that in order for things to go well, we must seek the advice of the professionals, the experts.

While there are people who can contribute to us, whether by providing information or offering suggestions, the reality is that you know what is going to work for you and for your business more than any so-called expert. Would you be willing to acknowledge and trust your knowing? Would you be willing to follow it even when it doesn't make sense to others?

3. Get the Information you Need

Following your intuition, trusting your knowing, does not mean that information is not required. When you find yourself feeling frustrated or upset, more than likely there is information that you need that you don't currently have. Get that information. Ask questions. Find the people who have the experience you require and ask them what they know. Listen, gather the information, and stay in your awareness all at the same time. As people are sharing with you what they know, you will have a sense of what to do with that information. Follow that. Allow others to contribute to you and never give up you and what you know in the process.

You have the ability to create your workplace in whatever way you would like it to be. It's truly up to you. When you honour you by trusting and following your awareness, everything around you begins to change.

Simone Milasas is a director of multiple companies and the Worldwide Coordinator of Access Consciousness™. She is a business mentor and specializes in enabling business owners to create businesses which operate from the 'Joy of Business'. She presents her 'Joy of Business' programs internationally and online. Website: http://www.accessjoyofbusiness.com

inSPIRIT | review

FROM GRIEF TO GODDESS

Published by Animal Dreaming Publishing

AUTHORED BY JUDE GARRECHT

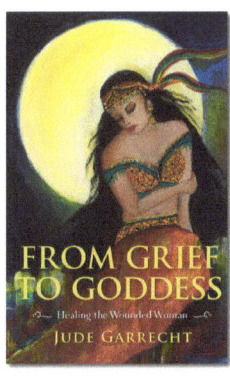

Jude Garrecht has written an honest and raw account about living with and healing from grief in all its facets after the ending of a fourteen year relationship.

Jude writes in such a way you immediately feel like she is a close and personal friend and you journey with her as she goes through grief's many stages, ultimately coming to accept the understandings and wisdom that grief can and does offer.

Gentle, flowing and easy to read, you feel nurtured as Jude shares lessons, meditative stories, affirmations as well as effective life and coping tools that she draws upon from her spiritual practice. You will quietly rejoice as Jude's deep connection with Spirit unfolds in these teachings and returns her to the Goddess within herself.

The accompanying Healing Cards can be purchased additionally to the book and be used as an empowering healing tool if you are yourself healing from a difficult time or would like to work with the affirmations that are featured in *'From Grief To Goddess'* book.

THE RELUCTANT PSYCHIC

Published by Universal LifePsycle

AUTHORED BY DEBBIE BOZICEVIC-MEWES

Author Debbie Bozicevic-Mewes shares her very personal journey into Mediumship and her Spiritual awakening with The Reluctant Psychic

Calling forth experiences which began seemingly without reason or explanation, we find Debbie opens her heart with her spiritual transformation and life's journey through marriage, parenthood and divorce, finding Spirit and love again along the way.

Throughout all of it, the author's insights and learnings in regards to communicating with Spirit are offered, making The Reluctant Psychic a worthwhile read for anyone who may find themselves walking a similar path, where natural psychic abilities are making themselves known. With the uncertainty that this all too common road can bring, this book will leave you with clarity and the sense of knowing you are not alone.

Advertise with Us

Advertise with inSpirit Magazine for :

- Best price value advertising,
- Your targeted market
- Cross promotion with Facebook and our email database

Contact us today at email: mail@inspiritpublishing.net

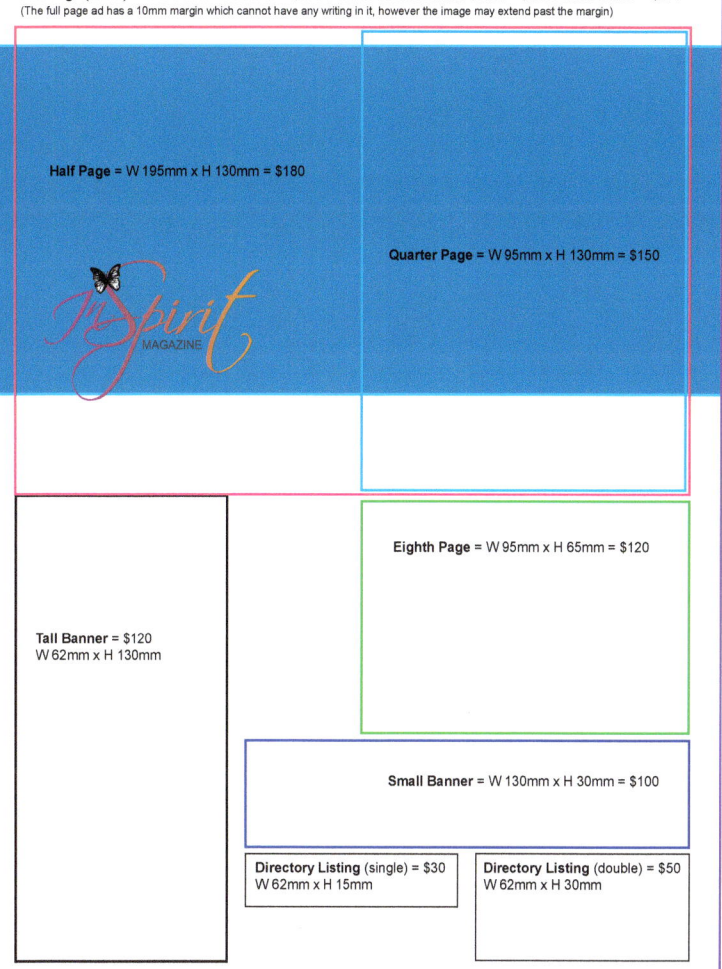

Full Page (Letter) = W 215mm x H 280mm = $210 / **Inside Front** or **Back Cover** = $240 / **Back Cover** = $270
(The full page ad has a 10mm margin which cannot have any writing in it, however the image may extend past the margin)

Half Page = W 195mm x H 130mm = $180

Quarter Page = W 95mm x H 130mm = $150

Eighth Page = W 95mm x H 65mm = $120

Tall Banner = $120
W 62mm x H 130mm

Small Banner = W 130mm x H 30mm = $100

Directory Listing (single) = $30
W 62mm x H 15mm

Directory Listing (double) = $50
W 62mm x H 30mm

inSPIRIT | Directory

AROMATHERAPY

THE SCENTED LOTUS
Boutique Aromatherapy Store
www.thescentedlotus.com

ARTWORK

NICOLLE POLL
Artwork by Nicolle - Oracle Cards, Animal Magick Series, Soul Journey Portraits
E: artworkbynicolle@bigpond.com
FB: www.facebook.com/ArtworkByNicolle

NICOLA MCINTOSH
Graphic Design, Fairy & Fantasy Art, Oracle Cards & Writer
www.nicolamcintosh.com

ASTROLOGERS

DAVID WELLS
Teacher, Qabalist, Astrologer, Author & Past Life Therapist
www.davidwells.co.uk

CRYSTAL SHOPS

JOPO FENG SHUI & CRYSTALS
2 Revesby Road, Revesby NSW
T: +612 9785 0798

SPIRIT STONE
For crystals & new age supplies
www.spiritstone.com.au

MAGICAL TOOLS

NATASHA HEARD
Blessed Branches
www.blessedbranches.com

GEM~MER
Cryshell Magic
www.cryshellmagic.com.au

NUMEROLOGY

AMANDA COPPA
Crystal Healer, Numerology & Astrology
www.facebook.com/cosmiccodes

PERSONAL GROWTH

KYE CROW
Wunjo Crow – Sacred Clothing, Animal Sanctuary & Sacred Journey into the Animal Realm workshops
www.camelcampsanctuary.com
www.facebook.com/Wunjocrow

PSYCHICS & MEDIUMS

KERRIE WEARING
Author, Soul Coach & Medium
www.psychicmedium.com.au

SCIENCE & SPIRITUALITY

BRENDAN D. MURPHY
Author - The Grand Illusion
www.brendandmurphy.net

SHAMANISM

LAURA NAOMI
Consultations, Workshops & Seminars
www.laura-naomi.com

STORYTELLING & FOLKLORE

REILLY McCARRON
Faerie Bard, Folklorist & Storyteller with Harp
www.faeriebard.com
E: info@faeriebard.com
F: Faerie Bard

RADIO SHOWS

 www.ghostsofoz.com

Would you like your listing included here? Email us at mail@inspiritpublishing.net for details.

Festival of Dreams

ancient wisdom embracing modern living

DARE TO DREAM AWAKE

Two massive days of rippling spine chilling heart energy, inspiring exhibitors, world renowned healers, international celebrity medium Lisa Williams, seminars and workshops, psychic readings, soulful entertainment, heartfelt meditations and more – all to elevate and celebrate life.

SAT 23rd and SUN 24th AUGUST, 2014

Sydney's Hordern Pavilion

Volume 7 Issue 2
The Scentual Divinities Issue
www.inspiritmagazine.com